First published in Great Britain in 2005 by Hamlyn
This edition published in 2014 by Spruce,
a division of Octopus Publishing Group Ltd,
Endeavour House, 189 Shaftesbury Avenue, London WC2H 8JY
www.octopusbooks.co.uk
www.octopusbooksusa.com

An Hachette UK Company www.hachette.co.uk

Copyright © Octopus Publishing Group Ltd 2014

Distributed in the US by Hachette Book Group USA
237 Park Avenue, New York NY 10017 USA

Distributed in Canada by Canadian Manda Group
165 Dufferin Street, Toronto, Ontario, Canada M6K 3H6

ISBN 978 1 84601 478 9
A CIP catalogue record for this book is available from the British Library
Printed and bound in China

1 2 3 4 5 6 7 8 9 10

Recipes by Joanna Farrow
Consultant Publisher Sarah Ford
Photography Stephen Conroy
Design Eoghan O'Brien and Michelle Tilly
Production Controller Sarah Connelly

Notes

A few recipes include nuts or nut derivatives. It is advisable for those with known allergic reactions to nuts and nut derivatives and those who may be potentially vulnerable to these allergies, such as pregnant and nursing mothers, invalids, the elderly, babies, and children, to avoid dishes made with nuts and nut oils. It is also prudent to check the labels of prepared ingredients for the possible inclusion of nut derivatives.

The American Egg Board advises that eggs should not be consumed raw. This book contains some dishes made with raw or lightly cooked eggs. It is prudent for more vulnerable people such as pregnant and nursing mothers, invalids, the elderly, babies, and young children to avoid uncooked or lightly cooked dishes made with eggs.

Whole milk, fresh herbs, and large eggs should be used unless otherwise stated.

Ovens should be preheated to the specified temperature—if using a fan-assisted oven, follow the manufacturer's instructions for adjusting the time and the temperature.

Pumpkin

NOT JUST FOR HALLOWEEN AND THANKSGIVING!

spruce

Contents

introduction

The bright orange pumpkin, that distinctive symbol of fall, belongs to the family of cucurbits (*Cucurbitaceae*), trailing vine plants that include squashes, gourds, zucchini, gherkins, muskmelons, and watermelons. Strictly speaking, pumpkins are fruits rather than vegetables. The flesh has a mild, sweet flavor and is used for both sweet and savory dishes. The seeds can be toasted (see page 63) to make a crunchy, nutritious snack or a garnish for soups and salads. Pumpkin flowers are also edible.

Grown throughout much of the United States, pumpkins take 90–120 days to mature before ripening between late summer and late fall, hence their popularity at this time of the year. As well as being used in cooking—in pies, cookies, bread, stews, and soups to name a few—pumpkins are often used to decorate homes in the fall and winter, especially for Halloween and Thanksgiving. Miniature pumpkins are commonly used as ornaments and can often be seen in autumnal floral displays, while larger ones are hollowed out and carved to make cheery—or spooky—jack o'lanterns. The earliest use for pumpkins was as animal feed and they are still used as such today.

A HISTORY OF PUMPKINS

Pumpkins are thought to have originated in Central America thousands of years ago. Spanish and Portuguese adventurers first introduced the seeds to Europe in the 14th century and, as a result, pumpkins are now grown worldwide. Native Americans in North America had been growing and using pumpkins long before the arrival of colonial settlers in the early 17th century. Besides roasting and eating the pumpkin flesh and the seeds, they used flattened, dried strips of pumpkin shell for making mats, and whole dried pumpkin shells were used as bowls and containers.

Pumpkins also became important for the Pilgrims. This explains the role of pumpkin—usually in the form of pumpkin pie—in today's Thanksgiving celebrations, which annually commemorate the thanks offered to God by the Pilgrims in 1621 following their first successful harvest. The first pumpkin pies were in fact pumpkin shells filled with milk, pumpkin flesh, spices, and maple syrup and baked for hours in hot ashes.

The word "pumpkin" is thought to derive from the classical Greek word "pepon". Pronounced by the French as pompon, this was later anglicized to "pumpion", and in turn altered by the American colonists to "pumpkin."

PUMPKIN VARIETIES

Pumpkins come in myriad shapes, sizes, and varieties, the names of which are probably better known to gardeners than to cooks. Some varieties are better for carving, while others are better for cooking. The best-known varieties are bright orange, ribbed, and round (90 percent of these are sold for Halloween jack o'lanterns), but pumpkins also come in shades of white, yellow, peach, tan, and green, and also stripey combinations of these colors. Sizes range from mini pumpkins the size of a tennis ball that weigh less than 1 lb to jumbo fruits grown for competitions that can weigh over 1000 lb. The cultivation of these outsized pumpkins is a popular pastime and the gigantic monsters (usually of the Atlantic Giant variety) are judged at pumpkin weigh-offs around the country at harvest time. The current record stands at 1337.6 lb.

SELECTING AND STORING PUMPKINS

If you are buying a pumpkin for cooking rather than for decorative purposes, its shape is unimportant. However, it should feel heavy for its size and be free of blemishes and soft spots, which can cause it to spoil prematurely. Although big pumpkins are impressive to look at, the flesh from smaller-sized fruits (the so-called pie, sugar, or sweet pumpkins) is usually sweeter and less watery than that from very large ones. The green-stripey cushaw is a long-necked pumpkin with green stripes, whose unique texture makes it ideal for custards and pies.

If possible, choose a pumpkin with 1–2 inches of stem left, because pumpkins without stems decay more quickly. Miniature pumpkins like the Baby Boo and Jack-Be-Little should be used soon after harvesting or purchasing, but larger, whole pumpkins can be stored at room temperature for up to a month or in a cool dry place for 2–3 months. Once a pumpkin is cut open it is highly perishable. It needs to be tightly wrapped, refrigerated, and used within 5 days.

NUTRITIONAL BENEFITS

Pumpkins are 90 percent water and, like most fruits and vegetables, of great nutritional value. They are low in calories and rich in fiber, vitamins C and E, and potassium. Vitamins C, and E are powerful antioxidants that help protect the body against free radicals—the highly unstable molecules that cause both minor infections and serious degenerative diseases like cancer and heart disease—as well as conditions that come with premature aging. Pumpkin seeds are a good source of essential fatty acids, protein, iron, and zinc.

HALLOWEEN JACK O'LANTERNS

The practice of using pumpkins as lanterns at Halloween derives from an ancient Celtic tradition brought to America by Irish immigrants. All Hallows' Eve on October 31st marked the end of the Celtic year, and it was on this night that the Irish would place hollowed-out turnips, rutabagas, and beets with a light inside in porches and windows. These would welcome the spirits of ancestors into their homes and ward off evil spirits and a restless soul called Stingy Jack. The story goes that Stingy Jack was a miserable, mean drunk who played tricks on the Devil. When Jack died he was refused entrance to Heaven. The Devil also refused him entry into Hell, sending him away with only a burning lump of coal to light his way. Jack was therefore left to roam the dark world between the two and carried his burning coal inside a hollowed-out turnip. When the tradition came to America, the larger and more easily carved native pumpkin became the favorite choice for hollowing out and a candle replaced the burning coal. "Jack o'lantern pumpkin" is now a generic term for the deep orange varieties like the Connecticut Field, the traditional American pumpkin, which is used for making these lanterns. Such varieties have large cavities and thin walls, which make them ideal for carving. Look for a pumpkin with a flat bottom, a hard outer layer with no soft spots, and an intact stem that you can use as a handle for the lid.

To hollow out a pumpkin, first cut out a "lid" that can be replaced. Scrape out the seeds and strings, and scoop out the flesh using an ice-cream scoop, which is stronger than an ordinary spoon. Scrape the inside wall of the area to be carved to a thickness of 1 inch. To carve your pumpkin, make sure you use a sharp knife, always cutting away from your body and using a gentle but firm sawing action. You can carve your pumpkin freehand if you prefer but there are plenty of carving kits containing stencils and saws. A light coating of petroleum jelly applied to the cuts will help the pumpkin last longer. Alternatively, you can buy commercial pumpkin protector spray.

PUMPKIN PUREE

Since fresh pumpkins are available only in the fall and early winter, canned and frozen pureed pumpkin are the next best thing and are available all year round. Solid-pack canned puree with no added salt or sugar is just as tasty and nutritious as fresh pumpkin. However, it is easy to make your own puree, which can be kept in the freezer for up to six months ready for use in tarts, pies, and any other recipe that requires solid-pack canned pumpkin. You will need about 1 lb of raw, untrimmed pumpkin to make 1 cup of pumpkin puree.

First remove the stalk, then cut the pumpkin in half, using a sharp knife, and scoop out the seeds and strings. The pumpkin can be boiled, steamed, or baked before pureeing. To boil or steam the pumpkin, cut it into large chunks (peel the skin now if desired) and place it in a saucepan with about 1 cup of water. Cover and boil for 10–15 minutes or until tender, then drain. Alternatively, steam the pieces for 15–20 minutes. To bake the pumpkin, simply place the two halves, cut-side down, on cookie sheets and bake in a preheated oven at 350°F for 1 hour. When it is cool enough to handle, remove the pumpkin skin using a sharp knife. Work the flesh to a puree in a food processor or blender, or press through a strainer, or ricer.

Glossary

US	UK
all-purpose flour	plain flour
arugula	rocket
bacon slices	bacon rashers
beet	beetroot
bell pepper	sweet pepper
broiler	grill
confectioner's sugar	icing sugar
cornstarch	corn flour
cilantro	fresh coriander
cornstarch	cornflour
ground beef	minced beef
Lima beans	butterbeans
peanut oil	groundnut oil
scallions	spring onions
self-rising flour	self raising flour
semisweet chocolate	dark chocolate
shrimps	prawns
skillet	frying pan
sour cream	soured cream
superfine sugar	caster sugar
zucchini	courgette

Conversion Table

Standard American cup measurements are used in all recipes.

¼ cup = 60 ml (2 fl oz)
⅓ cup = 75 ml (3 fl oz)
½ cup = 120 ml (4 fl oz)
1 cup = 240 ml (8 fl oz)

PUMPKIN AND APPLE
SOUP

¼ stick (2 tablespoons) butter
1 large onion, roughly chopped
2 teaspoons chopped fresh thyme
2 small cooking apples, peeled, cored, and chopped
3 tablespoons dark brown sugar
2 tablespoons whole-grain mustard
1 small pumpkin (about 1½ lbs) peeled, seeded, and cut into chunks
4½ cups vegetable stock
½ cup crème fraîche
salt and freshly ground black pepper
pumpkin seeds, for sprinkling

1. Melt the butter in a large, heavy-based saucepan. Add the onion and thyme and cook gently, stirring frequently, until softened and beginning to color, about 5 minutes. Add the apples and sugar and fry gently for another 3 minutes.

2. Add the mustard, pumpkin, and stock and bring just to a boil. Reduce the heat, cover with a lid, and simmer gently for about 20 minutes until the pumpkin and apples are very soft and falling apart.

3. Transfer the pumpkin to a food processor or blender and blend until smooth, or use a hand blender and blend the soup off the heat but while still in the pan.

4. Stir in half the crème fraîche, season to taste with salt and pepper, and heat through gently. Ladle into soup bowls, spoon over the remaining crème fraîche, and serve sprinkled with pumpkin seeds.

Mashed
PUMPKIN
AND POTATOES
WITH GARLIC CRÈME FRAÎCHE

1 lb large potatoes, cut into chunks
salt
2 lb pumpkin, peeled, seeded, and cut into chunks
3 garlic cloves, crushed
½ cup crème fraîche
freshly ground black pepper

1. Put the potatoes in a large saucepan, cover with cold water, and add a little salt. Bring to a boil. Add the pumpkin and cook for 15–20 minutes until the potatoes and pumpkin are very tender. Drain well and return to the pan.

2. Mash the vegetables thoroughly with a potato masher. Add the garlic, crème fraîche, and a little salt and pepper and mash until smooth. Serve hot.

Pumpkin and beet RAVIOLI

WITH FRESH HERB BUTTER

2½ cups pasta flour, plus extra for dusting
2 large eggs
3 large egg yolks
2 tablespoons olive oil
¼ teaspoon salt
9 oz pumpkin, peeled, seeded, and finely grated
1 small raw beet (about 3 oz), peeled and finely grated
1 garlic clove, crushed
beaten egg white, for glazing
½ oz bunch of fresh herbs (chives, parsley, tarragon)
1 stick (½ cup) unsalted butter
1 scallion, finely chopped
finely grated zest of 1 lemon plus 2 teaspoons juice
salt and freshly ground black pepper

1. Make the pasta: Place the flour on a work surface and make a well in the middle. Break in the eggs, add the egg yolks, the oil, and salt. Lightly whisk the eggs with a fork, gradually bringing in the flour, then use your fingers to mix into a soft dough, adding a tablespoon of cold water if the dough feels dry. Once the dough is smooth and elastic, wrap in plastic wrap and chill for 30 minutes.

2. Mix the grated pumpkin and beet with a little salt and pepper and the garlic until smooth.

3. Cut the pasta dough in half and roll each half on a floured surface, each to a 13-inch square. Brush one square with the egg white. Place 25 teaspoons of the filling in five evenly spaced rows over the dough. Lay the second sheet of dough on top, pressing between each mound of filling. Use a sharp knife or pastry wheel to cut the ravioli into squares.

5. Discard any tough stalks from the herbs and chop finely. Melt the butter in a small pan and add the herbs, scallion, lemon zest and juice, and salt and pepper. Set aside.

6. Bring a large pan of salted water to a boil. Drop the ravioli into the pan, bring back to a boil and cook for 3 minutes. Drain and arrange on warm plates. Spoon over the herb butter and serve immediately.

PUMPKIN OVEN FRIES
WITH SPICY SALSA

3 lb wedge from a large pumpkin, seeded
1/3 cup olive oil
1 teaspoon mild chili powder
salt

Salsa
7 oz cherry tomatoes, halved, seeded and chopped
2 scallions, finely chopped
1 celery stick, finely chopped
4 tablespoons chopped fresh cilantro
4 tablespoons lime juice
2 teaspoons superfine sugar
salt and freshly ground black pepper

1. Cut the pumpkin into thin wedges and then cut away the skin. Cut each wedge into fries, about 1/2-inch thick. Mix the oil with the chili powder and salt. Toss with the pumpkin pieces and place on a baking sheet, spreading out to an even layer. Roast in a preheated oven at 400°F for about 30 minutes, turning the fries frequently until golden and just tender.

2. Meanwhile, make the salsa. Mix together the tomatoes, scallions, celery, cilantro, lime juice, sugar, and salt and pepper. Transfer to a small bowl and serve as an accompaniment to the fries.

PUMPKIN
FRITTERS
WITH SOUR CREAM

1 cup all-purpose flour
½ teaspoon baking powder
1 large egg
⅔ cup cold water
½ oz fresh herbs (parsley, rosemary, thyme)
⅔ cup sour cream
salt and freshly ground black pepper
oil, for deep frying
2 lb pumpkin, seeded and cut into ¾-inch thick wedges

1. Put the flour and baking powder in a mixing bowl. Make a well in the middle, add the egg and pour a little of the cold water into the well. Whisk together the egg and the water, gradually incorporating the flour to make a thick paste. Beat in the remaining water to make a smooth batter.

2. Chop the herbs finely and mix with the sour cream and a little salt and pepper. Transfer to a small serving dish.

3. Heat 2 inches of oil in a large, heavy-based saucepan until the oil sizzles when you spoon a little batter into it.

4. Dip each pumpkin wedge into the batter and carefully lower into the oil. Fry for 2–3 minutes until pale golden. Drain with a slotted spoon and place on a plate lined with paper towels while cooking the rest. Serve with the sour cream.

Prosciutto-wrapped PUMPKIN WEDGES

1¼ lb pumpkin, seeded
6 wafer-thin prosciutto slices (about 3 oz)
1 teaspoon finely chopped fresh rosemary
¼ cup lemon juice
⅓ cup walnut oil
salt and freshly ground black pepper

Tip

These little wraps make a great starter served on a bed of salad leaves, or you can make smaller ones for hors d'oeuvres.

1. Cut the pumpkin into six even-sized wedges, then cut each wedge in half. Cut away the skin. Blanch the pumpkin pieces in boiling, lightly salted water for 4–5 minutes until just tender. Drain and cool slightly.

2. Cut each prosciutto slice in half lengthwise. Loosely wrap each one around a wedge of pumpkin and place on a baking sheet.

3. Mix together the rosemary, lemon juice, oil, and a little salt and pepper and spoon the dressing over the pumpkin. Bake in a preheated oven at 425°F for about 8 minutes until the prosciutto is just starting to color. Serve the wraps warm with any juices spooned over them.

PUMPKIN AND
PEARL
ONIONS
IN BALSAMIC VINEGAR

1 lb pearl onions
⅓ cup olive oil
1½ lb wedge from a large pumpkin, seeded
2 tablespoons light brown sugar
2 bay leaves
⅓ cup raisins
½ cup balsamic vinegar
salt and freshly ground black pepper

1. Peel the onions but leave them whole. Put them in a baking pan in which they line the base in a single layer. Pour the oil over them and roast in a preheated oven at 375°F for 20 minutes until they begin to soften.

2. Meanwhile, cut away the skin from the pumpkin and cut the flesh into 1-inch chunks. Add to the pan with the sugar, bay leaves, raisins, vinegar, and a little salt and pepper. Stir the ingredients together until combined.

3. Cover with a lid or foil and bake for 30 minutes until the onions and pumpkin are tender. Remove the bay leaves and serve the vegetables warm or cold with cheese or cold cuts.

PUMPKIN AND BEAN PATTIES
WITH GUACAMOLE

2 lb pumpkin, seeded, and cut into large wedges
1 x 15 oz can red kidney beans, drained and rinsed
1 tablespoon chopped fresh cilantro
1 small red onion, finely chopped
1 large egg
1 cup breadcrumbs
vegetable or peanut oil, for frying

Guacamole
1 large ripe avocado
2 tomatoes, skinned
2 tablespoons lime juice
2 tablespoons sweet chile sauce
salt and freshly ground black pepper

1. Put the pumpkin wedges in a baking dish. Season lightly with salt and pepper and roast in a preheated oven at 400°F for about 40 minutes until just tender. Remove the skin.

2. Place the pumpkin flesh in a food processor and blend until broken into small pieces. Add the beans, cilantro, a generous half of the chopped onion, and salt and pepper to taste. Blend to a coarse paste. Add the egg and ½ cup of the breadcrumbs and blend quickly until just combined, so the mixture is still quite chunky.

3. Using tablespoons, divide the mixture into 8 pieces. Using your hands, shape each piece into a ball then flatten slightly into a cake. Turn the cakes in the remaining breadcrumbs until evenly coated.

4. To make the guacamole, halve and pit the avocado and scoop the flesh into a small bowl. Scoop the seeds out of the tomatoes and discard. Finely chop the flesh and add to the bowl. Mash lightly to make a chunky paste. Add the reserved onion, lime juice, chile sauce, and salt and pepper and stir well. Place in a small serving dish, cover with plastic wrap, and chill until needed.

5. Heat a thin layer of oil in a large skillet. Add the pumpkin patties and sauté gently for 2–3 minutes on each side until golden. Drain and serve with the guacamole.

Crab

AND PUMPKIN SALAD

13 oz wedge from a large pumpkin, seeded
3½ oz snow peas
½ bunch of scallions
¼ cucumber
3½ oz beansprouts
¼ cup pumpkin seeds
⅓ cup olive oil
2 garlic cloves, thinly sliced
1 small red chile, seeded and thinly sliced
2 teaspoons light brown sugar
¼ cup lime juice
7 oz white crabmeat
salt

1. Remove the skin from the pumpkin and cut the flesh into ¼-inch thick slices. Cut them into more manageable-sized pieces if they are very large.

2. Shred the snow peas lengthwise. Trim and thinly slice the scallions. Cut the cucumber into matchsticks. Put the snow peas, scallions, cucumber, beansprouts, and pumpkin seeds into a large bowl.

3. Brush a broiling pan with a little of the oil and broil the pumpkin slices, as many as you can fit at a time, until golden on each side, about 8–10 minutes. Drain and allow to cool.

4. To make the dressing, mix together the remaining oil, garlic, chile, sugar, lime juice, and a little salt. Scatter the pumpkin slices and crabmeat over the salad. Add the dressing and toss gently to serve.

Tip
This salad is best served very fresh. You can prepare the vegetables and mix the dressing in advance, but toss the ingredients together right before serving.

SPICY
SWORDFISH
AND **PUMPKIN PENNE**

2 swordfish steaks
2 tablespoons chile oil
10 oz pumpkin, peeled, seeded,
and cut into ½-inch thick cubes
6 oz penne pasta
2 tablespoons lime juice
1 teaspoon superfine sugar
small handful of flat-leaf parsley, chopped
salt

1. Pat the fish dry on paper towels, drizzle with 1 teaspoon of the oil and sprinkle with a little salt.

2. Heat the remaining oil in a skillet. Add the pumpkin pieces and sauté gently, stirring frequently, for 5 minutes until browned and just tender. While the pumpkin is frying, bring a saucepan of water to a boil and cook the pasta until just tender.

3. Remove the pumpkin from the skillet and set aside. Sauté the fish for about 3 minutes on each side until cooked through. Using two forks, break the fish into smaller pieces.

4. Drain the pasta and return to the saucepan. Add the fish, pumpkin, any cooking juices, lime juice, sugar, parsley, and a little salt. Toss the ingredients together and serve immediately.

Tip
As a variation, try using other firm-textured fish such as salmon or monkfish for this recipe.

Pumpkin GNOCCHI

WITH CHILE BUTTER

2 lb pumpkin
1 cup all-purpose flour
2 egg yolks
several large sprigs of thyme
1 stick (½ cup) butter
1 red chile, seeded and thinly sliced
2 tablespoons lemon juice
salt and freshly ground black pepper

Tip
As a variation, omit the chile and herbs
and serve the gnocchi lavishly sprinkled
with freshly grated Parmesan.

1. If using a whole pumpkin, pierce it in several places with a knife; alternatively wrap a pumpkin wedge in foil. Bake in a preheated oven at 400°F for about 50 minutes until completely tender. Cool slightly, then discard the seeds and skin and roughly chop the flesh.

2. Put the pumpkin flesh into a bowl and mash with a potato masher until smooth. Add the flour, egg yolks, and plenty of salt and pepper and beat until smooth.

3. Bring a large saucepan of salted water to a simmer. Remove the thyme leaves from the sprigs and put the leaves into a small pan with the butter, chile, lemon juice, and a little salt and pepper. Heat gently to melt the butter while cooking the gnocchi.

4. Take a tablespoonful of the gnocchi mixture and slide it into the pan of water with another spoon. Working quickly, add several more in the same way and cook until the gnocchi rise to the surface. Drain and place in a warm serving dish while cooking the rest in batches.

5. Spoon the chile butter over the gnocchi and serve hot.

Pumpkin, Ricotta,
AND SPINACH TART

1¾ cups all-purpose flour, plus extra for dusting
1 stick (½ cup) butter, chilled

Filling
14½ oz wedge from a large pumpkin, seeded
¼ stick (2 tablespoons) butter
1 onion, sliced
3 garlic cloves, sliced
3½ oz baby spinach leaves
3½ oz ricotta cheese
2 large eggs
⅓ cup light cream
salt and freshly ground black pepper

1. To make the pastry, put the flour in a food processor with a little salt. Add the butter, cut into small pieces, and blend until the mixture resembles breadcrumbs. Add 1–2 teaspoons cold water and blend to a dough. Knead lightly until smooth, then wrap in plastic wrap and chill for 30 minutes.

2. Roll out the pastry on a lightly floured surface. Use to line a 9-inch, round, loose-based tart pan and trim off any excess. Line the pastry shell with parchment paper and fill with pie weights. Bake in a preheated oven at 400°F for 15 minutes, then remove the weights and paper and cook for another 5 minutes. Reduce the oven temperature to 350°F.

3. For the filling, cut away the skin from the pumpkin and cut the flesh into ¾-inch chunks. Melt the butter in a frying pan and sauté the onion, garlic, and pumpkin for 5 minutes until just beginning to color. Add the spinach to the pan and stir into the vegetables until it wilts slightly. Empty the mixture into the pastry shell and spread in an even layer to the edges.

4. Place spoonfuls of the ricotta over the filling. Beat the eggs with the cream and season with salt and pepper. Pour over the tart and bake for about 25 minutes until golden and lightly set. Serve warm or cold.

GOAT CHEESE AND PUMPKIN
SOUFFLÉ

3 tablespoons butter
¼ cup all-purpose flour
¾ cup plus 1 tablespoon milk
½ teaspoon mild chili powder
5 large eggs, separated
3½ oz firm goat cheese, crumbled
8 oz pumpkin, peeled, seeded, and finely grated
salt

1. Use 1 tablespoon of the butter to thoroughly grease a 6-cup soufflé mold. Melt the remaining butter in a saucepan. Add the flour and cook, stirring, for 1 minute. Remove from the heat and gradually blend in the milk, stirring. Return to the heat and cook, stirring, until the sauce is very thick and bubbling. Cool slightly, then add the chili powder, egg yolks, grated pumpkin, and goat cheese.

2. Whisk the egg whites in a large bowl until stiff peaks form. Using a large metal spoon, fold a quarter of the whites into the sauce to lighten it. Pour the mixture onto the remaining whites and fold in until evenly combined. Place in the prepared mold, smoothing down so that the top is level.

3. Bake in a preheated oven at 350°F for 30 minutes until well risen and golden. Serve immediately with a green salad.

SWEET POTATO,
PANCETTA,
AND PUMPKIN STEW

2 lb wedge from a large pumpkin, peeled and seeded
1 teaspoon mild chili powder
1 lb sweet potatoes, scrubbed
1 eggplant (about 10 oz)
½ cup olive oil
3½ oz pancetta or bacon, diced
2 onions, chopped
4 garlic cloves, crushed
2 x 14-oz cans chopped tomatoes
¼ cup chopped fresh oregano
⅔ cup vegetable stock
salt and freshly ground black pepper

1. Cut the pumpkin into large chunks and toss the pieces in the chili powder. Cut the sweet potatoes into similar-size chunks. Cut the eggplant into small cubes.

2. Heat ¼ cup of the oil in a large, heavy-based saucepan. Add the pancetta and onions and sauté gently for 5 minutes until lightly browned. Add the eggplant and drizzle with the remaining oil. Cook gently for 5 minutes, stirring frequently.

3. Add the garlic, tomatoes, oregano, pumpkin, sweet potato, and stock to the pan, then season with salt and pepper. Bring to a boil. Reduce the heat, cover with a lid, and leave to simmer gently for about 30 minutes until the vegetables are tender but still retain their shape.

4. Check the seasoning and serve hot with rice, pasta, or whole-grain bread, or as an accompaniment to grilled sausages or barbecued meat.

Beef and Pumpkin
CURRY

⅓ cup vegetable oil
1 red bell pepper, seeded and cut into chunks
1 green bell pepper, seeded and cut into chunks
2 onions, sliced
1 teaspoon ground turmeric
2 tablespoons coriander seeds, lightly crushed
2 teaspoons superfine sugar
1½ lb lean stewing steak, cut into small chunks
3 garlic cloves, sliced
1 oz fresh root ginger, peeled and chopped
1 red chile, seeded and chopped
1 x 14-oz can chopped tomatoes
2½ cups beef or chicken stock
2 lb pumpkin, seeded
salt
crème fraîche, for serving

1. Heat the oil in a large, heavy-based saucepan. Add the bell peppers and sauté for 4–5 minutes until they start to color. Drain with a slotted spoon and set aside. Add the onions, turmeric, coriander, sugar, and beef and sauté gently for 5 minutes or until lightly colored.

2. Add the garlic, ginger, and chile to the pan and cook for 2 minutes, stirring. Add the tomatoes and stock and bring slowly to a boil. Reduce the heat, cover with a lid and simmer on the lowest heat for 1 hour until the beef is tender.

3. Meanwhile, cut away the skin from the pumpkin and cut the flesh into chunks. Add to the pan along with the reserved red and green bell peppers. Cook gently for 20 minutes until the pumpkin is very soft. Season with salt if necessary and serve with crème fraîche and basmati rice.

PUMPKIN AND LEEK PHYLLO STRUDEL

1¼ lb pumpkin, peeled and seeded
¾ stick (6 tablespoons) butter, plus extra for greasing
¾ cup coarse breadcrumbs
3 small leeks, sliced
7 oz mushrooms, sliced
½ cup crème fraîche
2 teaspoons hot horseradish sauce
4 oz phyllo pastry
pumpkin seeds, to sprinkle
salt and freshly ground black pepper

1. Cut the pumpkin into ½-inch cubes. Melt 2 tablespoons of the butter in a skillet and sauté the breadcrumbs for 3–4 minutes until crisp and golden. Remove and set aside.

2. Melt another 2 tablespoons of the butter and sauté the leeks and mushrooms for 5 minutes, stirring, until golden. Transfer to a bowl and mix with the chopped pumpkin and salt and pepper.

3. Combine the crème fraîche and horseradish.

4. Melt the remaining butter. Lay two sheets of phyllo on a work surface, overlapping slightly, to make an 18 x 12-inch rectangle. Brush with a little butter and cover with a second layer of pastry, arranging it differently so the edges are not in the same place. Brush with more butter and cover with a final layer of pastry.

5. Spread the pumpkin mixture over the pastry, within about 2 inches of the edges. Scatter with the breadcrumbs, then spoon the crème fraîche along the middle. Fold the short ends of the pastry over the filling, then roll up from one of the long sides. Carefully transfer the strudel, with the seam underneath, to a lightly greased cookie sheet. Brush the strudel with any remaining butter and sprinkle with the pumpkin seeds. Bake in a preheated oven at 400°F for 35–40 minutes until the pastry is a deep golden brown and crisp. Leave to cool slightly before slicing.

PUMPKIN
AND PINE NUT RISOTTO

1 lb pumpkin, seeded
3 tablespoons butter
2 tablespoons olive oil
½ cup pine nuts
1 onion, chopped
2 garlic cloves, crushed
1⅓ cups Italian risotto rice
⅔ cup white wine
3¾ cups hot chicken or vegetable stock
½ cup freshly grated Parmesan cheese
salt and freshly ground black pepper

1. Cut away the skin from the pumpkin and cut the flesh into ¾-inch chunks. Melt half the butter in a large, heavy-based saucepan with the oil and sauté the pumpkin for 3 minutes. Add the pine nuts and sauté for 2 minutes until pale golden. Drain with a slotted spoon and set aside.

2. Add the onion to the pan and sauté for 3–4 minutes until very soft. Add the garlic and rice and cook, stirring, for 1 minute. Pour in the wine and let it bubble until evaporated.

3. Add a little of the hot stock and cook, stirring, until it is absorbed. Add a little more stock and cook until absorbed. Continue cooking, gradually adding the remaining stock, for about 20 minutes, stirring until the risotto is thick and creamy but the grains retain a little texture. You might not need all the stock.

4. Return the pumpkin and the pine nuts to the pan with the remaining butter and half the Parmesan. Season with salt and pepper to taste and spoon the risotto onto plates. Serve sprinkled with the remaining Parmesan.

Moroccan
PUMPKIN AND LAMB
C O U S C O U S

1½ lb pumpkin, seeded
14 oz lean lamb (fillet or leg)
⅓ cup olive oil
1 large onion, chopped
1 teaspoon ground turmeric
½ teaspoon hot chili powder
1-inch piece of fresh root ginger, peeled and grated
1 cinnamon stick
3 garlic cloves, sliced
2 large carrots, sliced
2½ cups lamb or vegetable stock
1 x 15-oz can chickpeas, drained and rinsed
1⅓ cups couscous
small handful of cilantro, chopped
salt and freshly ground black pepper

1. Cut the pumpkin into chunky wedges and cut away the skin. Chop the flesh into small chunks. Trim any excess fat from the lamb and season lightly with salt and pepper.

2. Heat the oil in a large heavy-based saucepan. Add the onion and sauté gently for 3 minutes. Add the lamb and sauté for about 5 minutes until it starts to color. Stir in the spices, ginger, garlic, and carrots and sauté for 2 minutes.

3. Add the stock and bring slowly to a boil. Reduce the heat, cover with a lid, and simmer on the lowest possible heat for about 50 minutes until the lamb is tender.

4. Stir in the chickpeas and pumpkin and cook gently for 15 minutes until the pumpkin is tender, adding a little water if the stew starts to dry out.

5. While the pumpkin is cooking, put the couscous in a heatproof bowl and cover with boiling water. Cover with foil or a plate and leave for 5 minutes until the water has been absorbed. Lightly season the couscous with salt and pepper and fluff up with a fork.

6. Stir the cilantro into the stew, check the seasoning and remove the cinnamon stick. Serve the stew spooned over the couscous.

Pumpkin
POTATO
AND ONION PIE

2 lb large potatoes, peeled
2 lb pumpkin, peeled and seeded
1 large onion, thinly sliced
3 garlic cloves, crushed
1¼ cups heavy cream
½ cup milk
plenty of freshly grated nutmeg
salt and freshly ground black pepper

1. Cut the potatoes into ⅛-inch thick slices. Cut the pumpkin flesh into ⅛-inch thick slices. If the pumpkin slices are very long, cut them down so they are a similar size to the potatoes.

2. Bring a large saucepan of lightly salted water to a boil. Add the potato and pumpkin, return to a boil and cook for 2 minutes. Drain.

3. Arrange half the potato and pumpkin slices in a large, shallow baking dish. Scatter with the sliced onions, then with the remaining potato and pumpkin. Mix the garlic with the cream, milk, and salt and pepper in a jug and pour over the vegetables. Grate plenty of nutmeg over the surface and bake in a preheated oven at 350°F for about 45 minutes until the vegetables are tender and the surface is golden.

GINGERED Noodles
WITH PUMPKIN WEDGES
AND CILANTRO

1 lb pumpkin, peeled and seeded
2 tablespoons peanut or vegetable oil
4 oz rice stick noodles
1 oz fresh root ginger, peeled and grated
½ oz fresh cilantro
¾ cup coconut milk
2 teaspoons Thai fish sauce
salt

1. Cut the pumpkin flesh into small cubes, discarding the skin. Heat the oil in a skillet and sauté the pumpkin for about 5 minutes, stirring frequently, until lightly browned and tender.

2. Meanwhile, put the rice noodles in a large heatproof bowl, cover with boiling water, and leave for 4 minutes. Drain.

3. Add the ginger, cilantro, coconut milk, fish sauce, and a little salt to the pumpkin and heat through for 1 minute. Stir in the noodles until all the ingredients are thoroughly mixed together and serve.

Tip
This makes a quick, easy and surprisingly rich supper dish. If desired, sauté some thinly sliced chicken before frying the pumpkin or add some cooked shrimp with the coconut milk.

Chicken
IN A PUMPKIN SHELL

1 whole pumpkin, about 10–11 inches in diameter
6 skinned, boneless chicken breasts
½ cup all-purpose flour
¼ stick (2 tablespoons) butter
2 tablespoons olive oil
2 large onions, chopped
13 oz zucchini, thinly sliced
3 red bell peppers, seeded and sliced
4 garlic cloves, crushed
½ teaspoon saffron strands, crumbled
1 x 14-oz can coconut milk
⅔ cup chicken or vegetable stock
1 cinnamon stick, halved
2 tablespoons cardamom pods
salt and freshly ground black pepper

Tip

Once you've ladled out the chicken mixture you can easily scoop out the pumpkin from the shell. Serve with chunky, warm bread to complete the meal.

1. Pierce the pumpkin all around the top with a skewer (keep the piercing at the top to avoid liquid seeping out when serving). Bake in a preheated oven at 375°F for about 1 hour until the flesh feels quite tender when the top of the pumpkin is pierced with a knife.

2. Meanwhile, chop the chicken into small pieces. Season the flour with salt and pepper and use to coat the chicken. Melt the butter with the oil in a large heavy-based saucepan and sauté the chicken, in batches if necessary, until golden. Remove with a slotted spoon.

3. Add the onions, zucchini, and red bell peppers to the pan and sauté gently for 5 minutes, adding a little extra oil if necessary. Return the chicken to the pan with the garlic, saffron, coconut milk, stock, and spices. Bring to a boil, then reduce the heat, cover, and simmer gently on the lowest possible heat for 1 hour.

4. Cut out a lid from the cooked pumpkin and remove it carefully, because it will be very hot inside. Scoop out and discard the seeds. Season the chicken to taste with salt and pepper and ladle into the pumpkin shell to serve. Alternatively, put it back in a very low oven for up to 1 hour until ready to serve.

MAPLE
ROAST HAM
WITH CRUSHED PUMPKIN

2 lb piece country-cured ham
2 onions, halved
2 carrots, roughly sliced
2 celery sticks, roughly sliced
3 bay leaves
2½ lb wedge from a large pumpkin, peeled and seeded
¼ stick (2 tablespoons) butter, melted
¾ cup maple syrup
juice of 1 orange
salt and freshly ground black pepper

1. Soak the ham overnight in plenty of cold water. Drain and place in a deep, heavy-based saucepan. Tuck the onions, carrots, celery, and bay leaves around the ham and season with pepper. Add enough cold water to just cover the meat. Bring slowly to a boil, reduce the heat, and simmer very gently, covered, for 1 hour.

2. Meanwhile, cut the pumpkin flesh into large pieces. Cook in a saucepan of boiling, salted water for 10–12 minutes until just tender. Drain and return to the pan. Lightly butter a shallow baking dish.

3. Lightly crush the pumpkin pieces by pushing them against the side of the pan until they are broken up but not mashed. Transfer to the buttered dish, spreading in an even layer. Drizzle with the melted butter and season with plenty of salt and pepper.

4. When the ham is cooked, drain it, discarding the vegetables, and cut away the skin. Place in a shallow baking dish or small baking pan with the skinned side up. Brush the fat with maple syrup and pour the orange juice into the dish.

5. Bake in a preheated oven at 400°F for about 25 minutes, basting frequently with the maple syrup and orange juice until pale golden brown. When the ham is almost baked, broil the pumpkin for 5 minutes until it begins to brown. Thinly slice the meat onto plates, spoon any pan juices over it, and serve with the pumpkin.

Chocolate
AND **PUMPKIN**
SEED BROWNIES

10 oz semisweet chocolate, broken into pieces
1¾ sticks unsalted butter
3 eggs
½ cup superfine sugar
¾ cup self-rising flour
¾ cup pumpkin seeds
7 oz vanilla fudge, chopped into small pieces

Tip
When baked, the brownie surface should still feel quite soft because of the high sugar content. Don't be tempted to cook them for longer as this will spoil the texture of the brownies.

1. Grease a 11 x 8-inch shallow baking pan and line with parchment paper. Put the chocolate into a heatproof bowl and add the butter. Melt until smooth.

2. Beat together the eggs and the sugar. Beat in the melted-chocolate mixture. then stir in the flour and all but ¼ cup of the pumpkin seeds. Stir in the chopped fudge and pour into the pan, spreading it into the corners. Sprinkle with the reserved seeds.

3. Bake in a preheated oven at 375°F for about 35 minutes until the center feels just slightly firm. Leave to cool in the pan, then transfer to a board and cut into small squares.

LAYERED PUMPKIN
AND BANANA
TEABREAD

8 oz pumpkin, peeled, seeded, and diced
finely grated zest and juice of ½ lemon
¼ cup clear honey, plus extra for glazing
2 small ripe bananas
¾ cup superfine sugar
1½ sticks (¾ cup) unsalted butter, softened
3 eggs
2¼ cups self-rising flour
1 teaspoon baking powder

1. Grease a 2 lb loaf pan, and line with parchment paper. Cook the diced pumpkin a little boiling water for about 5 minutes or until tender. Drain the pumpkin and return to the pan. Mash with a potato masher until smooth. Stir in the lemon zest and juice and the honey.

2. Mash the bananas. Put the sugar, butter, eggs, flour, and baking powder into a mixing bowl and beat with an electric hand mixer for 2 minutes or until smooth. Stir in the bananas.

3. Spoon a third of the banana mixture into the pan and level the surface. Spread with half the pumpkin mixture. Spoon half the remaining banana mixture on top, then spread with the remaining pumpkin mixture. Finally add the remaining banana mixture and level the surface.

4. Bake in a preheated oven at 325°F for 1¼ hours or until risen and firm to the touch. Leave in the pan for 10 minutes, then transfer to a wire rack to cool. Drizzle the top of the cake with extra honey.

Seeded
PUMPKIN
BREAD

13 oz pumpkin, peeled, seeded and cut into small chunks
5 cups white bread flour, plus extra for dusting
1 teaspoon salt
½ teaspoon ground mixed spice
2 tablespoons light brown sugar
2 teaspoons dry yeast
⅔ cup milk, plus extra for brushing
pumpkin seeds, for sprinkling

1. Cut the pumpkin into small chunks, discarding the skin. Steam over a pan of simmering water until tender. Transfer to a food processor or blender and process to a smooth puree.

2. Put the flour, salt, spice, sugar, and yeast into a large mixing bowl. Add the pumpkin puree and milk and mix to a smooth dough using a round-bladed knife. If the dough feels a bit dry, add a dash more milk.

3. Turn out the dough onto a lightly floured surface and knead gently for about 10 minutes until the dough is smooth and elastic. Transfer to a lightly oiled bowl, cover with plastic wrap and leave to rise in a warm place until doubled in size, about 1 hour.

4. Lightly grease a large baking sheet. Turn out the dough onto a lightly floured surface and punch to deflate. Form loosely into an oval shape and transfer to a baking sheet. Cover with plastic wrap and leave to rise again until doubled in size.

5. Lightly brush the top of the bread with a little milk. Using a sharp knife, make several diagonal scores across the bread, then sprinkle with the pumpkin seeds. Bake in a preheated oven at 400°F for 35–40 minutes until deep golden brown and the base sounds hollow when tapped. Cool on a wire rack.

Tip
This golden, moist-textured bread is delicious served fresh with butter or accompanying soups and warming casseroles. It's also good toasted for breakfast.

BACON
AND PUMPKIN
MUFFINS

¼ cup olive oil
1 large onion, finely chopped
4 oz smoked bacon, diced
2 cups self-rising flour
½ cup cornmeal or fine polenta
2 teaspoons baking powder
10 oz pumpkin, peeled, seeded, and finely grated
3 eggs
1 cup milk

Tip

As a variation, omit the bacon and add ½ teaspoon chili powder when sifting the dry ingredients.

1. Line a 12-cup muffin pan with paper muffin cups.

2. Heat the oil in a skillet and sauté the onion and bacon for 5 minutes until lightly browned.

3. Sift the flour, cornmeal, and baking powder into a large mixing bowl. Stir in the onion, bacon, and grated pumpkin. Beat the eggs with the milk and add to the bowl. Mix until just combined.

4. Divide the mixture among the paper cups and bake in a preheated oven at 400°F for 20–25 minutes or until risen, golden, and just firm. Transfer to a wire rack to cool. Serve buttered.

WHITE CHOCOLATE CHIP
AND PUMPKIN COOKIES

1 stick (½ cup) unsalted butter, softened
½ cup superfine sugar
8 oz pumpkin, peeled, seeded, and finely grated
1 egg
1¼ cups old-fashioned oatmeal
1 cup self-rising flour
3½ oz white chocolate chips
confectioner's sugar, for dusting

Tip

As a variation, use semisweet or milk chocolate chips instead of the white ones. Alternatively, chop a bar of chocolate into small pieces and use instead of the chocolate chips.

1. Grease two baking sheets. Beat together the butter and sugar until creamy. Beat in the grated pumpkin, then the egg, oatmeal, flour, and chocolate chips.

2. Place teaspoonfuls of the mixture on the baking sheets and flatten them slightly with the back of a spoon. Bake in a preheated oven at 350°F for about 20–25 minutes until risen and pale golden. Leave on the baking sheets for 2 minutes, then transfer to a wire rack to cool. Dust lightly with the confectioner's sugar.

Decorated PUMPKIN COOKIES

¾ cup plus 2 tablespoons unsalted butter
3 cups all-purpose flour, plus extra for dusting
1 teaspoon ground ginger
½ teaspoon grated nutmeg
½ small pumpkin, about ½ lb, peeled, seeded and grated
¾ cup confectioner's sugar
2 egg yolks
colored royal icing to decorate

1. Cut the butter into small pieces and put into a food processor with the flour, ginger, and nutmeg. Process until the mixture resembles fine breadcrumbs. Add the grated pumpkin and confectioner's sugar and blend briefly until combined. Finally, add the egg yolks and blend to form a soft dough. Wrap the dough in plastic wrap and chill for at least 2 hours.

3. Lightly grease two baking sheets. Roll out the dough on a lightly floured surface and,

using shaped cutters, cut out your cookies. Alternatively, you could create your own designs by making paper templates, placing them on top of the dough and then cutting round them with a knife.

4. Place the cookies slightly apart on the baking sheets and bake in a preheated oven at 350°F for 15–20 minutes, until golden. Transfer to a wire rack to cool.

5. Decorate the cookies with different colored royal icing. Spoon some colored icing into a piping bag with a decorating tip. Pipe around the edges of the cookies, then leave to dry. Fill in with the same colored icing using a larger tip on the piping bag. Allow to dry, then decorate the cookies with patterns of your choice. Leave to set for 1 hour before serving.

PUMPKIN MERINGUE PIE

8 oz prepared pie pastry
all-purpose flour, for dusting
1½ lb pumpkin, peeled and seeded
juice of 3 large oranges, plus the finely grated zest of 1
⅓ cup lemon juice
⅓ cup cornstarch
¾ cup water
1 cup, plus 2 tablespoons superfine sugar
3 egg whites

1. Roll out the pastry on a lightly floured surface and use to line a 9-inch round, loose-based tart pan with a depth of 1 inch. Line with parchment paper and pie weights and bake in a preheated oven at 400°F for 15 minutes. Remove the paper and weights and bake for another 5 minutes until golden.

2. Meanwhile, chop the pumpkin flesh into ½-inch cubes. Place the pumpkin in a saucepan with the orange zest and juice and the lemon juice. Bring to a boil, cover with a tight-fitting lid, and simmer gently for 10–15 minutes or until the pumpkin is tender. Allow to cool slightly, then place the pumpkin and juice in a food processor or blender and process until smooth. Return to the pan.

3. Blend the cornstarch with the water, then add to the pan with ⅓ cup of the sugar. Cook, stirring constantly, for about 3 minutes until the mixture is thick and bubbling. Pour into the pastry shell and level the surface.

4. Whisk the egg whites in a bowl until stiff. Gradually whisk in the remaining sugar, a little at a time and whisking well between each addition. Spoon the meringue over the filling and swirl with an offset spatula. Return to the oven for another 5–8 minutes until lightly browned. Allow to cool in the pan before serving.

Pumpkin amaretti
CHEESECAKE

7 oz amaretti or almond macaroons
3 tablespoons unsalted butter, plus extra for greasing
14 oz regular cream cheese
⅓ cup superfine sugar
2 eggs
2 teaspoons vanilla extract
⅔ cup heavy cream
14 oz pumpkin, peeled, seeded, and finely grated
½ cup golden raisins

1. Grease a 7-inch springform pan and line the sides with a strip of parchment paper.

2. Break 3 oz of the cookies into chunky pieces. Put the remainder in a plastic bag and crush them with a rolling pin. Melt the butter and stir in the crushed cookies until coated. Put the crushed cookies in the springform pan and press down in an even layer.

3. Beat the cream cheese in a bowl to soften it, then beat in the sugar, eggs, vanilla extract, and cream. Add the grated pumpkin, golden raisins, and broken cookies and stir until evenly mixed.

4. Pour the mixture onto the cookie base. Bake in a preheated oven at 325°F for 35–40 minutes until the center of the cheesecake feels just set. Allow to cool in the pan, then chill until ready to serve.

Tip
The golden raisins add pockets of sweetness that combine perfectly with the pumpkin, but for a nutty flavor, substitute ½ cup roughly chopped walnuts or pecans.

RHUBARB,
GINGER AND
PUMPKIN
C R U M B L E

1¼ lb pumpkin, seeded
13 oz rhubarb
½ cup light brown sugar
2 pieces crystallized ginger from a jar,
plus ⅓ cup of the syrup

Topping
1 cup all-purpose flour
½ cup ground almonds
1 stick (½ cup) unsalted butter
¼ cup light brown sugar
whipped cream, for serving

1. Cut the pumpkin into small chunks, discarding the skin. Trim the rhubarb and cut it into 1-inch lengths. Put the pumpkin and rhubarb into a saucepan with the sugar and heat gently for 4–5 minutes until the rhubarb juices start to run.

2. Thinly slice the ginger and add with the syrup to the pan. Place in a shallow baking dish.

3. To make the topping, put the flour and almonds in a food processor. Add the butter, cut into small pieces, and process until the mixture resembles breadcrumbs. Add the sugar and process in until the mixture starts to cling together slightly. Empty the mixture over the pumpkin and rhubarb and spread it to the edges of the dish.

4. Bake in a preheated oven at 400°F for about 30 minutes until the crumble is golden. Serve with whipped cream.

SERVES 10 • PREPARATION TIME: 20 MINUTES • COOKING TIME: 1 HOUR 10 MINUTES

Classic
PUMPKIN PIE

10 oz prepared pie pastry
all-purpose flour, for dusting
2 lb pumpkin, peeled, seeded , and roughly chopped
⅔ cup light brown sugar
2 pieces crystallized ginger from a jar, chopped
1 teaspoon ground cinnamon
2 eggs, beaten
⅔ cup heavy cream
confectioner's sugar, for dusting

Tip

Stir a little orange liqueur or brandy into some lightly whipped cream as an accompaniment.

1. Roll out the pastry on a lightly floured surface and use to line a 10-inch round, loose-based tart pan with a depth of 1½ inches. Line with parchment paper and pie weights and bake in a preheated oven at 400°F for 15 minutes. Remove the paper and weights and bake for another 5 minutes. Reduce the oven temperature to 350°F.

2. Steam the pumpkin chunks over a pan of gently simmering water for about 20 minutes until just tender. Remove from the heat and allow to cool slightly.

3. Place the pumpkin flesh in a food processor or blender and add the sugar, ginger, cinnamon, and eggs. Process to a smooth puree. Place the puree in a bowl and stir in the cream. Carefully pour into the pastry shell and bake for 30 minutes or until the pie is still slightly wobbly in the middle.

4. To give your pie that extra special touch, cut out leaves from any leftover pastry and place around the top edge of the pie. These can be cooked at the same time as the pie on a separate baking sheet for 10 minutes, or until golden brown. Dust with confectioner's sugar and serve warm or cold with heavy cream.

Sweet
PUMPKIN
FRITTERS
WITH SPICED VANILLA CREAM

⅔ cup heavy cream
1 teaspoon vanilla extract
½ teaspoon ground cinnamon
4 teaspoons superfine sugar
1½ lb pumpkin, peeled and seeded
2 tablespoons lemon juice

Batter
¾ cup all-purpose flour
2 tablespoons superfine sugar
2 eggs, separated
½ cup cold water
vegetable or peanut oil, for frying
extra superfine sugar, for dusting

1. Lightly whip the cream in a bowl with the vanilla, cinnamon, and 2 teaspoons of the sugar until soft peaks form. Transfer to a small serving dish and chill.

2. Slice the pumpkin flesh into chunky pieces, about ¾-inch wide. Toss in a bowl with the remaining sugar and the lemon juice.

3. For the batter, put the flour and sugar in a mixing bowl. Add the egg yolks and the cold water. Whisk to a smooth batter. Whisk the egg whites until peaks form, then fold into the batter with a large metal spoon.

4. Heat 1½ inches of oil in a heavy-based skillet until a teaspoonful of the batter sizzles and rises to the surface. Drop several of the pumpkin pieces into the batter and then lift out with a fork so the excess batter falls back into the bowl. Lower the battered pumpkin pieces carefully into the oil. Sauté for 2–3 minutes until golden. Drain on paper towels while cooking the rest.

5. Sprinkle with extra sugar and serve with the spiced vanilla cream.

Cinnamon
AND PUMPKIN
PANCAKES
WITH GINGERED CRÈME FRAÎCHE

2 pieces of crystallized ginger from a jar, finely chopped
1 cup crème fraîche
1 lb pumpkin, peeled, seeded, and cut into small chunks
2 eggs
1 cup all-purpose flour
1 teaspoon ground cinnamon
½ cup light brown sugar
vegetable or peanut oil, for shallow frying

Tip
Spoon maple syrup over the pumpkin pancakes as an alternative to the gingered crème fraîche.

1. Mix together the crystallized ginger and crème fraîche and put into a small serving dish.

2. Steam the pumpkin over a pan of gently simmering water for about 20 minutes until just tender. Allow to cool slightly then place in a food processor or blender and process to a smooth puree.

3. Add the eggs, flour, cinnamon, and sugar and process until smooth.

4. Heat a little oil in a large, heavy-based skillet. Place several spoonfuls of the mixture in the pan, spacing them slightly apart, and sauté gently until golden on the bottom. Turn the pancakes over and cook until just firm. Transfer to a warm plate while cooking the remaining batter. Serve warm with the gingered crème fraîche.

STICKY PUMPKIN AND BANANAS
WITH VANILLA ICE CREAM

14 oz pumpkin, peeled and seeded
3 tablespoons unsalted butter
2 tablespoons superfine sugar
finely grated zest and juice of 1 small orange
2 large bananas, each cut diagonally into quarters
¼ cup golden raisins
8 scoops of vanilla ice cream, slightly softened

1. Cut the pumpkin flesh into ¼-inch thick slices. Melt the butter in a skillet and sauté the pumpkin slices for 2–3 minutes on each side until lightly browned and softened.

2. Add the sugar and heat gently, stirring, until the sugar dissolves. Cook for about 1–2 minutes until the sugar starts to color.

3. Add the orange zest and juice, bananas, and golden raisins and cook gently for 2 minutes, stirring. Spoon over the ice cream in shallow bowls.

Caramelized PUMPKIN
WITH COCONUT RICE PUDDING

¾ cup pudding rice
1 x 14-oz can coconut milk
1 cup milk
2 bay leaves
¼ cup superfine sugar

Pumpkin

13 oz pumpkin, peeled and seeded
3 tablespoons unsalted butter
3 tablespoons superfine sugar

1. Put the rice in a heavy-based saucepan with the coconut milk, milk, bay leaves, and sugar. Bring slowly to a boil, stirring. Reduce to the lowest possible heat, partially cover with a lid, and simmer very gently for 30 minutes, stirring frequently, until the rice is tender and the mixture is thickened and pulpy. Add a little more milk if the pudding starts to dry out.

2. While the rice is cooking, cut the pumpkin flesh into ¼-inch thick slices.

Blanch the slices in boiling water for 2 minutes until softened but not falling apart. Drain.

3. Melt the butter in a skillet. Add the sugar and cook, stirring, until the sugar dissolves, then cook without stirring until the mixture starts to brown. Add the pumpkin slices and cook gently, turning the pumpkin in the buttery syrup until tender, about 3 minutes.

4. Remove the bay leaves once the rice is cooked. Spoon the rice into bowls and top with the pumpkin slices and syrup.

Tip

The bay leaves aren't essential in the rice pudding but they do give it a lovely aromatic flavor. Leave them out if you prefer. Keep an eye on the rice when you start cooking it because the milk can boil over if set on too high a heat.

PUMPKIN
AND APRICOT
CONSERVE

6 oz dried apricots, pitted and quartered
½ cup fresh orange juice
1½ lb pumpkin, peeled and seeded
1¼ cups superfine sugar

Tip
Serve this sweet conserve-like jam with bread or toast, or as a topping for yogurt. Alternatively, warm through and serve with ice cream.

1. Put the apricots and orange juice in a bowl, cover with plastic wrap and leave in a cool place overnight until the apricots absorb most of the juice.

2. Cut the pumpkin into small cubes. Put them in a heavy-based saucepan with the apricots, juice, and sugar and heat gently, stirring, until the sugar dissolves. Cook gently, uncovered, for about 25 minutes until the pumpkin is tender and the syrup thickened. Transfer to a clean jar or bowl and allow to cool completely. This conserve can be stored in the refrigerator for up to 2 weeks.

PUMPKIN AND RAISIN CHUTNEY

2 lb pumpkin, peeled and seeded
1 large onion, chopped
1 large cooking apple, cored and grated
1¼ cup raisins
1¾ cups white wine vinegar
1½ cups light brown sugar
1½ oz fresh root ginger, peeled and grated
2 teaspoons salt
2 cinnamon sticks, halved
2 tablespoons coriander seeds, lightly crushed

Tip

To sterilize glass jars, thoroughly clean the jars, removing any old labels, and heat in a low oven at 300°F for 15 minutes. Alternatively, use jars straight from a hot dishwasher cycle.

This quantity makes a small amount of chutney but can easily be doubled. You should increase the cooking time slightly.

1. Cut the pumpkin into ¾-inch chunks, and put it in a large, heavy-based saucepan and add all the remaining ingredients. Bring to a boil, stirring frequently. Reduce the heat and cook gently, uncovered, for about 45 minutes until the chutney is thick and pulpy. To check whether the chutney is cooked, draw a wooden spoon through the mixture—it should leave a clean trail on the base of the pan that slowly disappears.

2. Spoon the chutney into sterilized jars and cover with waxed discs and lids. Store in a cool place for a month before using.

Turkish PUMPKIN CANDY

2 lb wedge from a large pumpkin, peeled and seeded
⅔ cup light brown sugar
¼ cup water
¼ cup rosewater
2 tablespoons lemon juice
½ cup pistachio nuts, roughly chopped, skins removed

Tip
This makes a delicious sweet treat served with a swirl of thick yogurt or lightly whipped cream.

1. Cut the pumpkin into large chunks. Place in a heavy-based saucepan and add the sugar and water. Heat gently, stirring, until the sugar dissolves. Cook, uncovered, over a gentle heat for about 25 minutes, stirring frequently, until the pumpkin is very tender and the syrup is very thick.

2. Stir in the rosewater and lemon juice and serve sprinkled with the pistachio nuts.

Toasted PUMPKIN SEEDS

¼ stick (2 tablespoons) unsalted butter
1 cup pumpkin seeds
¼ cup sunflower seeds
1 teaspoon ground cinnamon
¼ cup superfine sugar

Tip
These mixed seeds make a great alternative to chips and nuts for nibbling. They're also good sprinkled over ice cream or scattered onto breakfast cereals.

1. Melt the butter in a large skillet. Add the pumpkin seeds and sunflower seeds, cinnamon, and sugar.

2. Cook over a gentle heat, stirring constantly, for 2–3 minutes until the sugary butter has turned into a caramel and the seeds are beginning to pop.

3. Transfer to a bowl and allow to cool. Mix with a fork to break up any seeds that may have stuck together.

INDEX